How To Start And Operate A Successful Catfish Farming Business For Profits

By

Benadine Nonye Nduagu

(www.Agric4Profits.com)

How To Start And Operate A Successful Catfish Farming Business For Profits

Catfish farming is a lucrative business in the aquaculture industry. It involves the breeding, rearing, and harvesting of catfish in an artificial pond or tank.

If you are interested in starting a catfish farming business, here are the practical steps involved:

Step 1: Research and Planning

The first step in starting any business is to research the industry and plan your business. This involves understanding the market demand, production costs, and regulations, and identifying potential customers.

You should also create a business plan that outlines your goals, financial projections, and marketing strategies.

For example, you can research the current demand for catfish in your area, the production costs involved, and the regulations you need to follow.

You can also plan your business by creating a business plan that outlines your goals, financial projections, and marketing strategies.

Step 2: Site Selection

Select a suitable site for your catfish farm. It should have a reliable source of water, preferably from a borehole or stream.

The site should be flat and well-drained to prevent flooding. Also, ensure that the location is accessible for transporting your catfish products.

Selecting a suitable site for a catfish farm is crucial to the success of your business. Site selection is a critical step in the catfish farming business.

By following these proper steps, you can select a suitable site that meets the requirements for pond construction, water quality, accessibility, and environmental regulations.

Here are the proper steps for site selection:

1. Conduct a site survey: The first step is to conduct a site survey to identify potential locations for your catfish farm. This involves inspecting the site for soil type, water availability, accessibility, and topography.

You can also consider factors such as climate, environmental regulations, and proximity to markets.

2. Soil quality: The soil quality of the site is important for pond construction and the growth of your catfish. Clay soil is ideal for catfish farming as it retains water and prevents seepage. Avoid sites with sandy or rocky soils that do not hold water.

3. Water quality and availability: Catfish require clean and well-oxygenated water to thrive. Therefore, the availability and quality of water are crucial factors to consider when selecting a site.

A reliable source of water, such as a borehole or stream, is essential for your catfish farm. You should also test the water quality for pH, temperature and dissolved oxygen levels.

4. Accessibility: The site should be easily accessible for transporting your catfish and supplies. It should have good road networks and be located close to markets, hatcheries, and feed suppliers.

5. Topography: The site should be flat or have a gentle slope to prevent water runoff and flooding. Avoid sites with steep slopes or valleys as they can be difficult to manage and prone to flooding.

6. Security: The site should be secure to prevent theft or damage to your catfish. You can install fencing or security cameras to protect your investment.

7. Environmental regulations: Before selecting a site, ensure that you comply with environmental regulations such as water use permits and waste disposal requirements. You can consult with your local environmental agency to obtain the necessary permits.

Step 3: Pond or Tank Construction

Catfish can be grown in ponds or tanks, depending on the scale of your operation. Construct your pond or tank with a dimension of 10 meters in length, 4 meters in width, and 1.5 meters in depth.

For example, you can construct your pond using concrete or clay soil. Ensure that your pond or tank has a secure fence to prevent predators from accessing your fish.

Constructing a suitable pond or tank is one of the critical steps in setting up a catfish farm. Constructing a pond or tank for your catfish farm requires proper planning, design, and implementation.

By following these proper steps, you can construct a suitable pond or tank that provides a comfortable habitat for your catfish to grow and thrive.

Here are the proper steps involved in a fish pond or tank construction:

1. Site selection: The first step is to select a suitable site for your pond or tank. The site should have a flat topography, be free from flooding, and have access to a reliable source of water.

The location should also be easily accessible for transportation of materials and fish.

2. Pond design and dimension: The next step is to design your pond or tank. The standard dimension for a catfish pond is 10 meters in length, 4 meters in width, and 1.5 meters in depth.

The pond should be rectangular or square in shape and should have a total area of 40 square meters. The pond should also have a sloping bottom with a depth of 0.5 meters at the shallow end and 1.5 meters at the deep end.

3. Soil preparation: After selecting the site and designing the pond, the next step is to prepare the soil for pond construction. Clear the site of trees, bushes, and debris, and level the ground.

Remove the topsoil and stockpile it separately for later use. Excavate the pond to the required depth and shape, using heavy equipment such as excavators.

4. Pond lining: The next step is to line the pond or tank to prevent water seepage. The most common materials used for pond lining are concrete, bentonite clay, and plastic liners.

For example, if you choose to use concrete, you should reinforce the concrete with steel bars and mesh to ensure the strength of the pond.

5. Inlet and outlet structures: Install inlet and outlet structures in your pond or tank. The inlet structure should allow water to enter the pond, while the outlet structure should allow water to leave the pond.

Install a screen or mesh at the inlet and outlet structures to prevent predators and debris from entering the pond.

6. Water supply and drainage system: Install a reliable water supply and drainage system in your pond or tank.

The water supply system should deliver clean and well-oxygenated water to the pond, while the drainage system should remove excess water from the pond.

The drainage system should also be designed to prevent erosion and runoff.

7. Fencing: Install a secure fence around your pond or tank to prevent predators such as birds and mammals from accessing your catfish.

8. Pond preparation: Once the pond construction is complete, allow the pond to settle for at least two weeks.

After this period, you can fill the pond with water and add organic matter to stimulate the growth of microorganisms, which serve as a food source for your catfish.

Step 4: Water Management

Water quality is critical to the success of your catfish farming business. Ensure that the water source is free from pollutants and has the right pH level and temperature.

You should also ensure adequate water circulation and aeration to prevent oxygen depletion and algae growth. You can also use a water test kit to monitor the water quality regularly.

Water management is a critical aspect of catfish farming because it affects the health and growth of your fish. Proper water management involves maintaining suitable water quality, temperature, and oxygen levels in your pond or tank.

Water management is essential for the success of a catfish farming business. By following these proper steps, you can maintain optimal water quality, temperature, and oxygen levels in your pond or tank, which promotes the growth and health of your catfish.

Here are the proper steps involved in water management for a catfish farm:

1. Regular water testing: Test the water quality of your pond or tank regularly using a water testing kit. The tests should measure parameters such as pH, ammonia, nitrite, nitrate, and dissolved oxygen levels.

The results of these tests will help you to adjust the water quality to the optimal range for your catfish.

2. Monitoring water temperature: Catfish thrive in warm water, with a temperature range of 25-32°C. Monitor the water temperature in your pond or tank using a thermometer and adjust it using a heater or aeration system to maintain the optimal temperature range.

3. Oxygenation: Catfish require a high level of dissolved oxygen in the water to survive and grow. You can improve oxygenation by installing an aerator or diffuser in your pond or tank.

These systems create turbulence in the water, which increases oxygen diffusion into the water.

4. Water exchange: Water exchange involves replacing some of the pond or tank water with fresh water. This helps to dilute toxins and improve water quality.

The frequency of water exchange depends on the stocking density, feeding rate, and water quality. A general rule is to exchange 10-20% of the water volume every week.

5. Feeding management: Overfeeding can lead to poor water quality due to excess waste and uneaten food.

Feed your catfish according to their size and appetite and remove any uneaten food after feeding. This reduces waste and prevents the buildup of toxins in the water.

6. Algae and weed management: Algae and weeds can grow rapidly in your pond or tank, reducing water quality and oxygen levels.

Control algae and weeds by manually removing them, using herbicides, or stocking herbivorous fish that feed on them.

7. Disease prevention and treatment: Disease outbreaks can be devastating to your catfish farm. Prevent disease outbreaks by maintaining good water quality and hygiene, avoiding overcrowding, and quarantining new fish before introducing them to your farm.

Treat any disease outbreaks promptly using appropriate medication and following recommended dosages.

The recommended water levels for catfish depend on the species of catfish, their age, and the stage of their growth. Generally, catfish requires a specific range of water quality parameters to grow and perform optimally.

Maintaining the optimal water quality parameters is essential for the growth and performance of catfish in a catfish farm.

Monitoring these parameters regularly and making necessary adjustments can help catfish farmers maintain a healthy and productive environment for their fish.

The following are the recommended water levels for catfish optimal growth and performance:

1. Temperature: Catfish are cold-blooded animals and their body temperature is dependent on the temperature of the water they inhabit. The optimal water temperature range for catfish is between 75-85°F (24-29°C).

In this temperature range, catfish can maintain good health and exhibit good growth rates. If the water temperature falls below 60°F (15°C), the growth rate of catfish can be significantly reduced.

2. Dissolved Oxygen (DO): Adequate levels of dissolved oxygen are crucial for the survival and growth of catfish.

The optimal DO levels for catfish are between 5-7 mg/L. DO levels below 3 mg/L can cause stress and may even lead to fish mortality.

3. pH: The pH level of the water is another crucial factor that affects the growth and health of catfish.

The optimal pH range for catfish is between 6.5 - 8.5. Any significant deviation from this range can cause stress and reduce the growth rate of the catfish.

4. Ammonia and Nitrite: Ammonia and nitrite are toxic to fish, and high levels of these chemicals can cause stress and even lead to fish mortality.

The recommended levels of ammonia and nitrite for catfish are less than 0.5 mg/L and less than 0.1 mg/L, respectively.

5. Alkalinity: Alkalinity is the measure of water's ability to resist changes in pH. The recommended alkalinity levels for catfish are between 50-200 mg/L.

High alkalinity levels can lead to a rapid increase in pH, while low alkalinity levels can cause pH to drop rapidly.

6. Hardness: Hardness is the measure of the concentration of minerals in the water, mainly calcium and magnesium. The recommended hardness levels for catfish are between 50-150 mg/L.

7. Salinity: Catfish are freshwater fish and cannot tolerate high levels of salinity. Therefore, the recommended salinity level for catfish is zero.

Step 5: Stocking

Select healthy and disease-free catfish fingerlings from a reputable hatchery. Stock your pond or tank with a density of 1-2 fingerlings per square meter.

Ensure that your catfish feed on a high-quality diet to promote growth and prevent disease. For example, you can feed your catfish with commercial fish feed or homemade fish feed.

Stocking refers to the process of introducing young catfish into a pond or tank for growth and development. Proper stocking is critical to the success of a catfish farming business.

Stocking is a crucial step in catfish farming. By following these proper steps, you can ensure that your fingerlings are healthy, well-distributed, and growing well, which leads to a successful and profitable catfish farming business.

Here are the proper steps involved in stocking a catfish farm:

1. Selecting healthy fingerlings: Fingerlings are young catfish that are typically 2-4 inches in length. Select fingerlings that are healthy, active, and disease-free.

Avoid fingerlings that show signs of stress, such as lethargy, abnormal swimming behavior, or discoloration.

2. Determining stocking density: Stocking density refers to the number of fish per unit area of the pond or tank. The stocking density depends on factors such as pond or tank size, water quality, and management practices.

A general rule is to stock 1,000-2,000 fingerlings per acre of pond or 100-200 fingerlings per cubic meter of tank.

3. Acclimating the fingerlings: Before stocking the fingerlings, acclimate them to the pond or tank water gradually.

This reduces stress and helps them to adjust to the new environment. Place the fingerlings in a container filled with pond or tank water for 10-15 minutes.

Then, add a small amount of pond or tank water to the container every 5-10 minutes until the water temperature in the container is similar to that of the pond or tank.

4. Distributing the fingerlings: Distribute the fingerlings evenly across the pond or tank. This ensures that they have enough space to move around and access food.

Avoid overcrowding, as this can lead to poor water quality, disease outbreaks, and stunted growth.

5. Monitoring the fingerlings: Monitor the fingerlings closely after stocking to ensure that they are healthy and growing well.

Check their feeding behavior, growth rate, and disease symptoms. Make adjustments to water quality, feeding, and management practices as needed.

6. Feeding the fingerlings: Provide the fingerlings with a balanced diet that meets their nutritional needs. Feed them small amounts of commercial feed several times a day. Adjust the feeding rate based on their growth rate and appetite.

7. Harvesting the catfish: Harvest the catfish when they reach the desired size, typically 1-2 pounds for market-size fish. Drain the pond or tank and remove the fish using a seine or net. Transport them to a processing facility or sell them directly to customers.

Step 6: Catfish Feeding

Catfish feeds are available in various sizes and forms. Choosing the right feed size and feeding guide is essential for the proper growth and development of catfish on a catfish farm.

The feed size and feeding frequency will depend on the size of the catfish, their age, and the water temperature.

Choosing the right size of catfish feed and feeding guide is critical for the successful growth and development of catfish in a catfish farm.

By following the proper feeding guidelines, catfish farmers can ensure that their fish receive the necessary nutrients and achieve optimal growth rates.

Here's a detailed explanation of the different sizes of catfish feeds and the proper catfish feeding guide:

1. Starter Feed: Starter feed is typically given to catfish fry (baby catfish) from hatch to around four weeks of age.

This feed is designed to provide the necessary nutrients for the fry to grow and develop into fingerlings. The pellet size of the starter feed ranges from 0.5mm to 1.5mm.

2. Fingerling Feed: Fingerling feed is typically given to catfish from four weeks of age to around two months of age. The pellet size of fingerling feed ranges from 1.5mm to 3mm.

3. Juvenile Feed: Juvenile feed is given to catfish from two months of age to around six months of age. The pellet size of juvenile feed ranges from 3mm to 6mm.

4. Grower Feed: Grower feed is given to catfish from six months of age to maturity. The pellet size of grower feed ranges from 6mm to 9mm.

5. Finisher Feed: Finisher feed is given to mature catfish in the final stage of growth before harvesting. The pellet size of finisher feed ranges from 9mm to 12mm.

Proper Catfish Feeding Guide

1. Feed catfish 1-2 times daily, depending on their age and size. Fry and fingerlings should be fed small amounts of feed frequently throughout the day, while mature catfish can be fed larger amounts at longer intervals.

2. Do not overfeed catfish as this can lead to water quality problems and health issues. As a general rule, feed the catfish only what they can consume within 5-10 minutes.

3. Monitor water temperature, as this can affect the catfish's metabolism and feeding behavior. In colder water temperatures, catfish may eat less, while in warmer water temperatures, they may eat more.

4. Choose a high-quality catfish feed that meets the nutritional requirements of the fish at each stage of growth.

5. Keep the feeding area clean and free of debris to prevent waste buildup and maintain water quality.

6. Regularly monitor the catfish for signs of health problems and adjust feeding accordingly.

7. Gradually adjust feeding amounts and pellet sizes as the catfish grow and develop.

Step 7: Catfish Disease Control

Monitor your catfish regularly for signs of disease and take appropriate measures to prevent or treat the disease.

Ensure that your pond or tank is free from pollutants and that you maintain good water quality. For example, you can use a pond net to remove any dead fish or debris from your pond or tank.

Catfish disease control is an important aspect of catfish farming that helps to ensure the health and well-being of the fish, and ultimately the success of the farm.

Catfish disease control is a critical aspect of catfish farming that helps to ensure the health and success of the farm.

By following these proper steps, farmers can prevent disease outbreaks, identify and treat diseases promptly, and maintain healthy and productive fish.

Here are the proper steps involved in catfish disease control:

1. Prevention: The best way to control catfish diseases is to prevent them from occurring in the first place.

This can be achieved through good management practices, such as maintaining good water quality, providing proper nutrition, and minimizing stress on the fish.

Implement biosecurity measures such as proper disinfection of tools, equipment, and facilities.

2. Identification: Regular monitoring and observation of the fish is necessary to detect any signs of disease early.

Look for signs of abnormal behavior, such as lethargy, loss of appetite, and discolored skin or fins. Work with a veterinarian to determine the cause of the symptoms and diagnose the disease.

3. Treatment: If a disease is detected, prompt treatment is necessary to prevent it from spreading and causing significant losses. The appropriate treatment depends on the specific disease and its severity.

Treatment may involve the use of antibiotics, vaccines, or other medications. Follow all label instructions and obtain the appropriate permits to use these medications.

4. Record-keeping: Keep detailed records of disease outbreaks, treatments, and preventive measures taken.

This information helps in the identification of trends and the development of a plan for future prevention and control of diseases.

5. Disposal: Proper disposal of dead fish and waste is important to prevent the spread of disease. Dead fish should be removed and disposed of promptly.

Do not allow them to remain in the water for an extended period. Wastes should also be disposed of properly and not allowed to accumulate in the pond or tank.

6. Quarantine: If a disease is detected, quarantine affected fish to prevent the spread of the disease to healthy fish.

Separate the affected fish in a separate tank or pond and avoid handling them with equipment or tools that have been used in other areas of the farm. Disinfect all equipment and tools used in the quarantine area.

Catfish diseases are common in catfish farms and can lead to significant losses if not properly managed.

Managing catfish diseases in a catfish farm requires regular monitoring and prompt treatment of infected fish. Proper sanitation, water quality management, and good feeding practices can help prevent the spread of diseases in catfish farms.

If you suspect that your catfish may have a disease, it is important to consult with a veterinarian or an aquatic animal health specialist to determine the appropriate treatment.

The following are some of the most common catfish diseases and their treatments:

1. Aeromonas Infection: Aeromonas is a bacterial infection that affects the skin and internal organs of catfish. Symptoms include lethargy, loss of appetite, and open sores on the skin.

The treatment for Aeromonas infection involves the use of antibiotics such as oxytetracycline, florfenicol, or sulfadimethoxine.

2. Columnaris Disease: Columnaris is a bacterial infection that affects the skin and gills of catfish. Symptoms include white or gray patches on the skin, frayed fins, and difficulty breathing.

The treatment for columnaris disease involves the use of antibiotics such as oxytetracycline, florfenicol, or sulfadimethoxine.

3. Ichthyophthiriasis (Ich): Ich is a parasitic infection that affects the skin and gills of catfish. Symptoms include white spots on the skin, increased mucus production, and rapid breathing.

The treatment for Ich involves the use of formalin, copper sulfate, or malachite green.

4. Edwardsiella Septicemia: Edwardsiella is a bacterial infection that affects the internal organs of catfish. Symptoms include lethargy, loss of appetite, and open sores on the skin.

The treatment for Edwardsiella septicemia involves the use of antibiotics such as oxytetracycline, florfenicol, or sulfadimethoxine.

5. Motile Aeromonad Septicemia (MAS): MAS is a bacterial infection that affects the internal organs of catfish. Symptoms include lethargy, loss of appetite, and open sores on the skin.

The treatment for MAS involves the use of antibiotics such as oxytetracycline, florfenicol, or sulfadimethoxine.

6. Enteric Septicemia of Catfish (ESC): ESC is a bacterial infection that affects the digestive system of catfish. Symptoms include lethargy, loss of appetite, and distended abdomen.

The treatment for ESC involves the use of antibiotics such as oxytetracycline, florfenicol, or sulfadimethoxine.

7. Whirling Disease: Whirling disease is a parasitic infection that affects the nervous system of catfish. Symptoms include whirling, loss of balance, and difficulty swimming.

The treatment for whirling disease involves the use of formalin, copper sulfate, or malachite green.

Step 8: Harvesting

Harvest your catfish when they reach a marketable size of 500-1000g. You can use a seine net or a cast net to catch the fish. Drain the water from the pond or tank and transport your catfish to the market.

For example, you can transport your catfish in a fish transport tank or a plastic bag filled with oxygen.

Harvesting is the process of removing the catfish from the pond or tank for sale or processing. Proper harvesting techniques ensure that the fish are handled in a manner that minimizes stress and maintains their quality.

Proper harvesting techniques are crucial to the success of a catfish farming business. By following these proper steps and processes, farmers can ensure that their fish are handled in a manner that maintains their quality and minimizes stress, resulting in healthy and profitable catfish.

Here are the proper steps and processes involved in the harvesting of catfish on a catfish farm:

1. Planning: Proper planning is necessary to ensure a successful harvest. Plan the harvest date and time, and ensure that you have all the necessary equipment and supplies. Consider factors such as weather conditions, transportation, and market demand.

2. Water management: Before harvesting, reduce the water level in the pond or tank to make it easier to catch the fish. Gradually reduce the water level over several days to avoid stressing the fish.

3. Catching: Use a seine net or fishing rod to catch the fish. For a seine net, spread the net across the pond or tank and slowly draw it towards the shore. For a fishing rod, use bait to attract the fish and reel them in.

4. Sorting: Sort the fish according to size and quality. This helps to ensure that you can sell or process them separately based on market demand. Use a sorting table or container to separate the fish.

5. Processing: If the fish are to be processed, such as gutted and cleaned, do so promptly after harvesting to maintain their quality and freshness. Use clean and sharp knives and cutting boards to minimize damage to the fish.

6. Transporting: Transport the fish to the processing facility or market using a clean and properly ventilated truck or container. Avoid overcrowding and excessive handling of the fish, as this can cause stress and reduce their quality.

7. Record-keeping: Keep detailed records of the harvested fish, including the number, size, and quality. This information helps to track performance, estimate yields, and plan for future harvests.

Step 9: Marketing and Sales

Identify potential customers for your catfish products. You can sell your catfish to local markets, restaurants, and hotels. You can also create an online presence to market your catfish products.

For example, you can create a website or social media account to promote your catfish products. You can also offer discounts or promotions to attract new customers.

Marketing is an essential aspect of catfish farming that involves promoting and selling the catfish to customers. Proper marketing techniques can help to increase demand for the fish and improve profitability.

Proper marketing techniques are crucial to the success of a catfish farming business. By following these proper steps and processes, farmers can effectively promote and sell their catfish to customers, resulting in increased demand, profitability, and success.

Here are the proper steps and processes involved in marketing catfish on a catfish farm:

1. Identifying the target market: Determine the target market for your catfish, such as local grocery stores, restaurants, or individuals. Understand their preferences and needs to better promote your product.

2. Branding: Develop a brand for your catfish that sets it apart from competitors. Consider aspects such as packaging, labeling, and advertising to create a unique brand image.

3. Pricing: Set a competitive and profitable price for your catfish. Consider factors such as the cost of production, market demand, and competitors' prices.

4. Promotion: Promote your catfish through various channels, such as social media, flyers, or word-of-mouth. Use pictures and videos to showcase your catfish and emphasize its quality and freshness.

5. Sales channels: Choose the most effective sales channels for your catfish, such as direct sales to consumers or selling to wholesalers. Consider factors such as transportation costs, volume of sales, and the target market.

6. Distribution: Establish a distribution system to get your catfish to the customers. Consider factors such as transportation, storage, and handling to ensure that the fish remain fresh and of high quality.

7. Customer service: Provide excellent customer service to build a positive reputation and attract repeat customers. Respond promptly to customer inquiries and complaints, and be willing to make changes to improve the quality of your catfish.

8. Record-keeping: Keep detailed records of your sales, expenses, and profits. This information helps to track performance, identify areas for improvement, and make informed decisions for future marketing efforts.

Step 10: Catfish Processing and Storage

Catfish processing involves a series of steps that transform the live fish into a finished product that is ready for sale and consumption.

Catfish processing involves a series of steps and processes that transform live fish into a finished product that is ready for sale and consumption.

These steps include harvesting, live hauling, grading and sorting, cleaning and dressing, filleting, packaging, quality control, and storage and distribution.

Proper handling, sanitation, and quality control measures are essential to ensure that the finished product is of consistent quality and meets industry standards and regulations.

The following are the steps and processes involved in catfish processing:

1. Harvesting: The first step in catfish processing is harvesting. This involves catching the live fish from the ponds using nets or other harvesting equipment.

2. Live Hauling: After harvesting, the live fish are transported from the ponds to the processing facility using live hauling equipment. The fish are typically transported in tanks or containers filled with water to ensure their survival during transportation.

3. Grading and Sorting: Once the live fish arrive at the processing facility, they are graded and sorted based on size and weight. This allows for more efficient processing and ensures that the finished product is of consistent quality.

4. Cleaning and Dressing: The next step in catfish processing is cleaning and dressing the fish. This involves removing the scales, gutting the fish, and removing the head and tail. The fish are then washed and placed in containers for further processing.

5. Filleting: After cleaning and dressing, the fish are filleted. This involves removing the bones and cutting the fish into fillets of a consistent size.

6. Packaging: Once the fish has been filleted, they are packaged for sale and distribution. This can include vacuum-sealed bags, frozen packaging, or other packaging methods depending on the intended use of the fish.

7. Quality Control: Throughout the processing and packaging process, quality control measures are implemented to ensure that the finished product meets industry standards and regulations.

This can include visual inspections, microbiological testing, and other quality control measures.

8. Storage and Distribution: Finally, the finished product is stored in refrigerated or frozen storage facilities before distribution to retail outlets, restaurants, and other customers.

In conclusion, catfish farming requires careful planning, management, and marketing to succeed. These practical steps are crucial to the success of your catfish farming business.

By following these steps above and taking proper care of your catfish, you can start a profitable catfish farming business.